le monde minuscule
I. la danse du microbe

engraved by Osho Endo

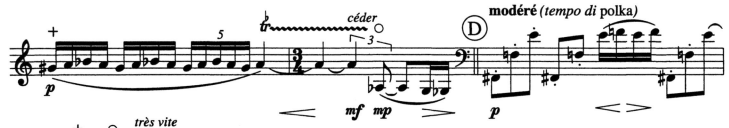

II. le petit Americain

* up a quarter tone

le monde minuscule - 3

III. l'insecte et le pachiderme

* gradually increasing in speed while simultaneously closing the hand in the bell,
  achieving a full hand-stopped position for the written G.

le monde minuscule - 4

IV. e-mail

V. poussières de sable sur flocons de neige